REAL
Christianity

Experience *Real Christianity* with your small group.

THE OFFICIAL SMALL GROUP STUDY GUIDE

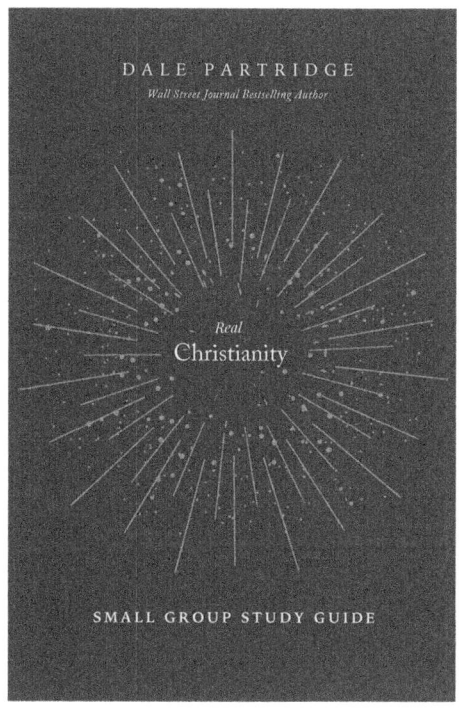

AVAILABLE AT

RelearnChurch.org/RCSG

What if the culture's definition of success is God's definition of failure?

ALSO AVAILABLE FROM DALE PARTRIDGE

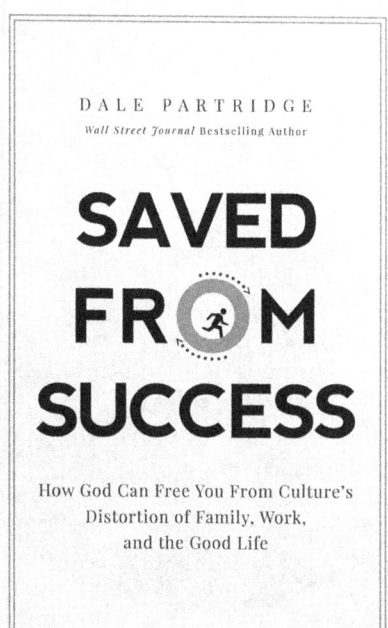

AVAILABLE AT

RelearnChurch.org/Success

Build a Biblical Marriage

DALE & VERONICA PARTRIDGE'S SIX-WEEK
MARRIAGE MENTOR PROGRAM—A RAW,
BIBLE-BASED, ONLINE COURSE FOR CHRISTIAN
COUPLES AND SMALL GROUPS.

AVAILABLE AT

UltimateMarriage.com

Listen to Podcasts? Join Dale & Veronica each Wednesday

LISTEN ON ITUNES, YOUTUBE, GOOGLE PLAY, SPOTIFY & MORE

AVAILABLE AT

RelearnChurch.org/Listen

REAL *Christianity*

HOW TO BE BOLD FOR CHRIST
IN A CULTURE OF DARKNESS

DALE PARTRIDGE

RELEARN PRESS

To Matt, thank you for your committed discipleship. I am more like Christ because of you.

© 2019 by Relearn Church. All rights reserved.

No portion of this book may be reproduced, stored in a retrieval system, or transmitted in any form or by any means— electronic, mechanical, photocopy, recording, scanning, or other—except for brief quotations in critical reviews or articles, without the prior written permission of the publisher.

Published in Bend, Oregon, by Relearn Church.

Scripture taken from the New King James Version®. Copyright © 1982 by Thomas Nelson. Used by permission. All rights reserved.

For information, please contact us through our website at RelearnChurch.org.

Table of Contents

About the Author	15
Critical Introduction: For Who and for What?	19
Belief in Christ Doesn't Make You Christian	23
If Some Are False Then None is True	31
Dedication & Death	49
Abide or Depart	61
Do You Really Love Jesus?	71
Costless Christianity	83
Eternally Secure or Relationally Contingent?	101
Hate the Captor Not the Captive	119
Conclusion: Real Christianity	135
Bringing the Church Back to the Bible	143

Author · Dale Partridge

Widely known as an online thought leader on faith, family, and church; Dale is also a Bible teacher and writer read by millions. He and his wife Veronica produce a weekly podcast titled *Real Christianity*, lead a marriage program at UltimateMarriage.com, and operate a church planting ministry at RelearnChurch.org.

Dale studied biblical theology at Western Seminary and now serves alongside a network of house churches in the Pacific Northwest. At the core, their mission is to bring the church back to the Bible. Together, they live with their children on a small farm in Bend, Oregon.

RelearnChurch.org   @DalePartridge   /DaleJPartridge

"The most dangerous prayer a human being could ever pray, 'Lord, make me like Christ. I don't care if you have to dethrone me, I don't care if you have to tear apart my ministry, I don't care if you have to destroy me, I don't care what happens—make me like Jesus Christ!' It's practically calling a death sentence upon yourself. But then again, 'unless a grain of wheat falls to the ground and dies, it abideth alone, but if it dies, it bringeth forth much fruit.'" [1]

PAUL D. WASHER

CRITICAL INTRODUCTION
—

For Who and For What?

Several studies have shown that somewhere between 50–60% of Americans identify themselves as Christian. While these polls bring clarity regarding the total professions of faith in my country, there is no study which measures these professions against the standards set forth in the Bible. If there were, I expect that number would be significantly less.

What I'm alluding to is the gap between what the Bible says about following Christ and the people who claim to follow Christ.

Now even the most devout Christians have a gap. We all fall short, yet grace abounds. That said, our love for

Christ and desire for personal holiness should drive us to close this gap—not with a Pharisaical posture, but a Spirit-filled soul.

That is what this book is about.

Real Christianity is a book for Christians looking to be more like Christ. It is not an out-looking book aimed to highlight the contrast between "real Christians" and "fake Christians." It is an *in-looking* book aimed to highlight what the Bible says about being a real Christian and a careful examination of *your* personal walk with Jesus. In other words, I did not write this to accuse the lukewarm, but to rouse the faithful.

PRACTICAL EXPECTATIONS

If you're anything like me, you don't like long books. Condensing content is an art. Writing in a way that cuts the clutter while leaving the essentials is key. This was my aim for this book. It's short, concise, and bold. While you will see a connection between the content of each chapter, this book has less of a unified thread than most. Instead, I have chosen to briefly tackle a variety of topics that, together, form the fullness of what it means to follow Christ according to Scripture.

At the end of each chapter, you will see a few reflection questions to help you examine your heart—and determine if you're embracing the truth.

The entire book is less than 15,000 words (about the length of an extensive magazine article). The average reader can complete it in one hour and thirty minutes. In my personal experience, books of this nature lend themselves well to discussion amongst others, which is why we have chosen to develop a powerful small group study guide that can be purchased at: RelearnChurch.org/RCSG.

Lastly, it's my sincere hope that this book is not only consumable, practical, and shareable, but that it becomes a resource for anyone looking to gain clarity in their faith and resurrect their zeal for Christ and His Kingdom.

CHAPTER 01
—

Belief in Christ Doesn't Make You Christian

As you continue through this manuscript, you will see my thesis for this book: relationship is the linchpin to *real* Christianity. Without relationship, the topic of salvation becomes a difficult discussion. Without relationship, the Bible is reduced to mere moralism and philosophy. Without relationship, we attempt to *do* instead of rest in what's been *done*.

Sadly, however, the church has diminished the definition and expectation of a relationship with Christ from a committed participatory and pursuant bond to merely believing in His existence.

But is belief in Jesus the only thing God is looking for? Are the eternal benefits of the Gospel—the reconciliation of humanity and a holy God—hinged simply on the sole requirement of belief in Jesus Christ?

Romans 10:9 declares, "If you confess with your mouth the Lord Jesus and believe in your heart that God has raised Him from the dead, you will be saved." Now, does the word *confess* simply mean to verbally state "Jesus is real," in a room full of people? I mean, do you *really* think that's all God is looking for? Of course not! The Greek word for confession is *homologeo*, and is defined as "authentically agreeing, admitting, and acknowledging."

Ultimately, salvation isn't simply dependent on belief in Jesus' existence. Jesus' own brother, the Apostle James, knew this when he wrote, "Even the demons believe—and tremble." (James 2:19). In truth, salvation (and a fruitful Christian life) is dependent on three things: belief that Jesus is the Christ, a willingness to make Him Lord, and a recognition that God raised Jesus

Ultimately, salvation isn't simply dependent on belief in Jesus' existence. Jesus' own brother, the Apostle James, knew this when he wrote, "Even the demons believe—and tremble."

#RealChristianity

from the dead. Together, these three postures create the bedrock for divine relationship.

The question you must ask yourself is this: Is Jesus Lord in your life or do you just believe in His existence? Is Christ your everything or is He just something? Have you made Him an unrivaled priority? Or is He simply convenient comforter, good philosophy, your framework for conservative politics, or someone who's there only when you need Him?

For many Christians, Jesus has been reduced from Lord to savior, comforter, provider, or whatever is a convenient bandage to the most painful element of their life at the time. However, that's simply a gross misunderstanding of who Jesus truly is. Let me explain using an analogy from my own life.

I love my wife. She's the "cook" and the "house cleaner" of our home. But I would never reduce her to just "cook" or "house cleaner." No. That would be demeaning. She's my wife! Cooking and cleaning are jobs, not identities—they're what she does for me but they are not who she is to me. Do you see the difference?

Similarly, "savior" or "comforter" or "provider" are things that Jesus does for us, but that's not simply who He is. Jesus is Lord. I believe the Scriptures support this identity, too. The word "Savior" is mentioned a mere 36 times in the entire Bible. The word "Lord" occurs 7,800 times! Where do you think God is placing the emphasis?

Jesus is Lord. And until we fully renounce our lives and relinquish the desire to direct our own paths in this world, we will not understand what it means to be a *real* Christian—a Christian who has died in the flesh, been born again of the Spirit, and who now walks by faith in a precious relationship with their Lord.

Reflection Questions

Have you truly made Jesus Lord in your life? If yes, please explain how you know this to be true. If not, please explain what has prevented you from doing so.

_____
_____
_____
_____
_____
_____
_____
_____
_____
_____
_____
_____
_____
_____
_____
_____

Allowing Christ to be Lord in every domain is an ongoing journey, are there any areas in your life that need to be further released to Him? Explain below.

CHAPTER 02
—

If Some are False Then None is True

We live in a time when many Christians, churches, and even entire denominations have begun to question the authority of Scripture. Pastors have found ways to dismiss doctrine through context, history, or audience.

For example, I've heard several Christians explain away the relevancy and doctrines of the entire book of 1st Corinthians. I recall a preacher once saying, "Remember, this was a letter written to Christians 2,000 years ago for a culture 2,000 years ago."

Ultimately, this does two things. First, this disposition

further advances the growing idea that when Scripture is tough on our flesh, we can always find a contextual angle to side-step its jurisdiction. Additionally, this posture implies that the words of that book (1st Corinthians) are not relevant or authoritative to a modern community of believers.

But that's a lie. In 1st Corinthians, Paul clearly states who he wrote his letter to—and it's not just for a distant Corinthian culture long ago. In verse two we see the letter's intended audience:

> *"To the church of God which is at Corinth, to those who are sanctified in Christ Jesus, called to be saints, with all who in every place call on the name of Jesus Christ our Lord, both theirs and ours."*
> —1 CORINTHIANS 1:2

Ultimately, there are four people groups Paul is writing to:

1. "The church of God which is at Corinth." Is that you? No.

2. "Those who are sanctified in Christ Jesus." Is that you? Well, if you call yourself Christian, absolutely.
3. Those who are "called to be saints." Again, is that you? I hope so.
4. "With **all** who in **every** place call on the name of Jesus Christ our Lord…" I hesitate to ask, but is this letter written only to the Corinthians? No. Is this letter written to you? Well, if you're part of the "all" and "every" category who calls on the name of "Jesus Christ our Lord" then, yes.

During my time in seminary, I had the privilege of studying hermeneutics. That's just a fancy word for people with more degrees than Fahrenheit, but the term simply means "the art and science of interpreting the Bible."

Now, I am in no way saying that elements like history, cultural context, or audience are unimportant. They are critical to understanding the content thoroughly. But those elements only *add* to the authority and depth of God's word—not *subtract* from it.

Another critical lesson captured during my graduate studies was the skill of separating prescriptive doctrine from descriptive history. Here's what I mean... Let's take the book of Acts for example, this is a historical account of what happened in the early church. It is not generally viewed as a doctrinal book of the Bible. While the Gospels and epistles of Paul (minus Philemon), James, Jude, Peter and John are generally viewed as prescriptive doctrinal books. Do you see the difference?

Let me explain further. In Acts 2, we see that the church sold all their possessions and considered everything they had to be common. That's what they did, but it's not necessarily what all Christians are commanded to do. It doesn't mean it's a sin to share everything you own, but there are simply no other commands in Scripture that prescribe that behavior.

Ultimately, Christians have to be capable of discerning the correct interpretation of the text, regardless of whether it's complex, unpopular, uncomfortable, or uncommon. In addition, we must look at the New Testament letters as universal truths that are to be applied locally in your own life and church.

The implication that 1st Corinthians doesn't hold any authority simply because of its timestamp would indicate that Paul was unaware that he was actually writing universal, divinely inspired Scripture. Is that true? Did Paul not know he was writing holy texts? I doubt it and here's why. In 1st Thessalonians 2:13 Paul writes:

> *"For this reason we also thank God without ceasing, because when you received the word of God which you heard from us, you welcomed it not as the word of men, but as it is in truth, the word of God, which also effectively works in you who believe."*

Later in this same book (5:27) he pens, "I charge you by the Lord that this epistle be read to all the holy brethren."

In 1st Corinthians 14:37 the Apostle continues with, "If anyone thinks himself to be a prophet or spiritual, let him acknowledge that **the things which I write to you**

"The Scriptures don't change; they change us. If we disagree with something we read in Scripture, it's not the Bible that needs to change—it's us."

#RealChristianity

are the commandments of the Lord." Ultimately, Paul addresses his own writings as a command of the Lord. Furthermore, Peter looks at Paul's writings as Scripture.

> *Therefore, beloved, looking forward to these things, be diligent to be found by Him in peace, without spot and blameless; and consider that the longsuffering of our Lord is salvation—as also our beloved brother Paul, according to the wisdom given to him, has written to you, as also in all his epistles, speaking in them of these things, in which are some things hard to understand, which untaught and unstable people twist to their own destruction, as they do also the rest of the Scriptures.* –2 PETER 3:14-16

Earlier in this epistle, Peter maintains this theme even about his own writings as he places them at equal status as the Old Testament Scriptures.

> *"Beloved, I now write to you this second epistle (in both of which I stir up your pure minds by way of reminder), that you may be mindful of the words which were spoken before by the holy prophets, and of*

> ***the commandment of us, the apostles of the Lord and Savior..."*** **–2 PETER 3:1-2**

The fact of the matter is this: The human writers of the New Testament knew who the true Author was behind their words. I think pastor Michael Youssef makes my point nicely when he says, "The Scriptures don't change; they change us. If we disagree with something we read in the Scriptures, it's not the Bible that needs to change—it's us."[2]

Fellow theologian Dustin Benge recently wrote, "There is no tension in Scripture. If we perceive tension, the tension is within us, not within the Scriptures."

God's Word is unchanging. It's immovable. Jesus Himself says in Matthew 24:35, "Heaven and earth will pass away, but My words will by no means pass away." *Real* Christians don't avoid the text because of its unpopularity or discomfort or difficulty within a modern culture. *Real* Christians embrace God's Word in all times, hoping that it will mature their faith and glorify God in the process.

ALL OR NOTHING

Biblical authority isn't all that's under attack in today's churches, so is biblical accuracy. What I mean by this is that many Christians don't even believe the entire Bible is true. As a result, they take a smörgåsbord approach to the Word of God which looks something like this:

"Well, I believe this is true... But I think that section over there is just a story and didn't *really* happen... And I don't understand what it's saying here so I'll disregard it... But hey, I like this stuff over here..."

In other words, we like the figurative principles but we don't like the literal truths. We like what's convenient but not what's convicting.

It's peculiar to me how many pastors dismiss difficult parts of Scripture—from the creation narrative and the Garden of Eden to Noah's flood and Jonah's time in the great fish. May I please remind you that these are all portions of God's story that Jesus personally mentions during His earthly ministry? In other words, are you really going to believe in Jesus, but not believe in Jesus'

Scripture doesn't become false, right doesn't become wrong, and truth doesn't become irrelevant just because certain passages aren't accepted by an individual pastor or church.

#RealChristianity

belief in the Scriptures?

Booker T. Washington, an African American advisor to various Presidents of the United States, wrote, "A lie doesn't become truth. Wrong doesn't become right. And evil doesn't become good just because it's accepted by the majority."³ Put differently, Scripture doesn't become false, right doesn't become wrong, and truth doesn't become irrelevant just because certain passages aren't accepted by an individual pastor or church.

When we take a dismissive approach with Scripture, we end up doing what Thomas Jefferson did with his Bible—he cut out what he didn't like and left the rest. This slippery slope approach causes a major league conflict with scriptures like 2 Timothy 3:16 where Paul declares, "All Scripture is given by inspiration of God, and is profitable for doctrine, for reproof, for correction, for instruction in righteousness, that the man of God may be complete, thoroughly equipped for every good work."

And when you combine that passage with the text in

Hebrews 6:18 that states, "It is impossible for God to lie.", it forces Christians to choose a side. Either you believe that *all* Scripture is without error, written by the inspiration of God (who cannot lie), or it's not.

But this journey of trusting God's Word is not for the faint of heart. In fact, Hebrews 11:16 tells us that believing in the unseen is inescapable, "But without faith it is impossible to please Him, for he who comes to God must believe that He is, and that He is a rewarder of those who diligently seek Him." While this is speaking directly to salvation, the principle reigns equally true in this discussion. That is to say, we will not fully understand everything we read. We must make room for faith or what theology calls "divine accommodation"—meaning intellectual compromise when heavenly ideas hold earthly ambiguity.

Thankfully, we serve a God who is very logical with us and has sufficiently revealed Himself in many pragmatic ways. Yet still, it requires faith, humility, and a decent tolerance for mystery to believe in the total accuracy of Scripture. We have to admit that we don't understand everything God has written. In fact, in Isaiah 55:8–9 God reminds us of this certitude, "For My thoughts are not your thoughts, Nor are your ways My ways,' says the Lord. For as the heavens are higher than the earth, So are My ways higher than your ways, And My thoughts than your thoughts."

The heart of the matter is this, we have an enemy who is always looking for ways to diminish the confidence humanity has in the Word of God. His first attempt as seen in the Garden of Eden (see Genesis 3:1) has remained his classic strategy, "Did God *really* say…" He knows he doesn't have to disprove God's word, he simply needs to birth doubt. It's an all-out assault to leave God's church divided, confused, unsure, fractured, and weak.

That said, in order to be bold for Christ in a culture of darkness, you must know where you stand. At times, you may feel like a rock in the midst of a rushing river—everything is against you but firm you stand. You may feel like a house in the midst of a turbulent storm—everything is against you but firm you stand.

You may even feel like a target in the midst of a culture war—everyone is against you but firm you stand.

This is the heart of a *Real* Christian—deep commitment to the Word of God. Men and women who are humble yet rigid, gentle yet bold, and meek yet strong.

REFLECTION QUESTIONS

Do you believe the Bible is true and without error? If not, what's preventing you from this belief?

Do you believe the Bible has the jurisdiction and authority to instruct you how to live, think, feel, and believe? If not, why?

If you answered yes to the previous two questions, how does this change your life, your marriage, your parenting, your leadership or view of God?

CHAPTER 03
—

Dedication & Death

Altars are everywhere in Scripture. In fact, they are mentioned over four hundred times in the biblical text. But we see this word *altar* first used in Genesis 8:20 when Noah leaves the ark and builds an altar in gratitude of God's justice and mercy. The concept of an altar, however, is seen even earlier in Scripture. In Genesis 4:3–4, we witness God requesting a presentation of offerings from both Cain and Abel. While the word *altar* isn't formally stated in the narrative, we can assume that both men placed their offerings on some form of an altar.

As we will learn, an altar in the Scriptures always

represents a place of dedication and death. The Old Testament, in fact, paints a beautiful spiritual story with these altars. Theologically speaking, an altar was a tool or expression to memorialize a significant moment with God. We see this with Abram (Genesis 12:7), Isaac (Genesis 26:24–25), Jacob (Genesis 35:3), David (1 Chronicles 21:26), and Gideon (Judges 6:24) who each built altars to mark and solemnize unique engagements with their Maker. In speaking to its purpose for dedication, God was keenly aware of our forgetfulness as humans and these physical altars became a visual memorial for personal reflection and a monument of reminder for future generations.

In speaking to its purpose for death, in Leviticus 17:11 God tells us, "For the life of the flesh is in the blood, and I have given it to you upon the altar to make atonement for your souls; for it is the blood that makes atonement for the soul."

Ultimately, God has declared that blood is required for the removal of our sin. In the days of Moses, it came from goats and calves and bulls. In the present, it has come from Jesus Christ Himself.

In the grand hour of Christ's crucifixion, the Lord fulfilled the ceremonial laws and the sacrificial system of the Old Covenant and birthed a New Covenant with His people.

> *"But Christ came as High Priest of the good things to come, with the greater and more perfect tabernacle not made with hands, that is, not of this creation. Not with the blood of goats and calves, but with His own blood He entered the Most Holy Place once for all, having obtained eternal redemption. For if the blood of bulls and goats and the ashes of a heifer, sprinkling the unclean, sanctifies for the purifying of the flesh, how much more shall the blood of Christ, who through the eternal Spirit offered Himself without spot to God, cleanse your conscience from dead works to serve the living God? And for this reason He is the Mediator of the new covenant, by means of death, for the redemption of the transgressions under the first covenant, that those who are called may receive the promise of the eternal inheritance.* –HEBREWS 9:11-15

The altar is a bloody place. For those who lived within the Old Covenant this was a structure made of stones. For Christ, it was a wooden cross. For us, it is within the inner room of our hearts—a place of our own spiritual dedication and death.

However, over the years, the church has distorted our understanding of the altar. It has been reduced from a place of full consecration and the flesh passing away, to a sort of repeat-after-me spiritual pledge. But if we look at the Scriptures, you'll never see this kind of altar call. You'll never see Jesus, or Paul, or anyone else for that matter, utter the words, "With everybody's head bowed and eyes closed, raise your hand and repeat after me if you'd like to accept Jesus into your heart."

While this approach is not sinful, we must ask if it's biblical or, at least, fruitful. As someone who has spent a fair amount of time studying the Bible, I can't help but believe the altar call (a.k.a. the invitation) experience that includes a softly strummed acoustic guitar with low lighting is more of an emotional tactic aimed at softening the expense of the altar than it is about

> "Jesus makes it profusely clear that there's no such thing as costless Christianity."

#RealChristianity

clarifying the real cost. But before you disagree, let's look at how Jesus Himself conducts an altar call in Luke 14:25–33.

> *"Now great multitudes went with Him. And He turned and said to them, 'If anyone comes to Me and does not hate his father and mother, wife and children, brothers and sisters, yes, and his own life also, he cannot be My disciple. And whoever does not bear his cross and come after Me cannot be My disciple. For which of you, intending to build a tower, does not sit down first and count the cost, whether he has enough to finish it—lest, after he has laid the foundation, and is not able to finish, all who see it begin to mock him, saying, 'This man began to build and was not able to finish'? Or what king, going to make war against another king, does not sit down first and consider whether he is able with ten thousand to meet him who comes against him with twenty thousand? Or else, while the other is still a great way off, he sends a delegation and asks conditions of peace. So likewise, whoever of you does not forsake all that he has cannot be My disciple.'"*

Dedication & Death

As you read this passage, it's easy to see that Jesus doesn't sugarcoat the cost, commitment, or consequences hidden behind the decision to come to the altar and follow Him. He's upfront and raw.

Out of His abundant grace and love, He makes it profusely clear that there is no such thing as costless Christianity. He isn't interested in winning people under false expectations. He wants you to know everything before you pick up your cross, die on that altar, are born again of the Spirit, and become His disciple.

But what I find so interesting about this passage is how Jesus drives the point home even further: "For which of you, intending to build a tower, does not sit down first and count the cost, whether he has enough to finish it…"

There's no bait-and-switch. There's no sales pitch. Jesus even encourages them to sit down and collectively consider the cost before making such a colossal commitment. Why? Because it's a life-altering decision (no pun intended), "Whoever of you does not forsake

Real Christianity: Chapter 03

all that he has cannot be My disciple."

Don't be a fool. If you follow Jesus, you will pay a price, you will die on an altar, but then you will truly live. Matthew 16:25 confirms this when the Lord tells us, "For whoever desires to save his life will lose it, but whoever loses his life for My sake will find it."

Bottom line: there's a cost to follow Christ. This has been evident throughout the ages. Western Christianity has tried to bury it under prosperity messages and celebrity pastor platforms, but the question Christians must ask themselves is, "Am I really willing to pay the price? Am I really willing to make Christ the priority of my life? Am I really willing to kill the desires of my flesh on an altar? Am I really willing to forsake all that I have to be His disciple?"

So, how does Jesus' altar call turn out in that passage? Interestingly, many walk away. Yet thousands still decide to follow Him. This Sunday, I'm guessing that you won't see many American mega church pastors model their altar call after Jesus' example. It's too risky. It's too costly.

Instead, we continue to fill churches with an attempt to sell Jesus. To talk about the positive and ignore the price—a format that's leaving people unsure of what they've signed up for. A format that's left many folks believing they're following Christ when in reality, they are still following themselves.

Reflection Questions

How did you come to Christ? Did you dedicate yourself and die to your will or have you learned that your flesh is still living, still leading, and still loving your sin?

_____
_____
_____
_____
_____
_____
_____
_____
_____
_____
_____
_____
_____
_____
_____

Have you met a Christian who has accepted the Gospel without understanding what it meant for their life? Have you seen them hobble along under confusion and conflict between their will and His? If so, what could you say to this person to help them understand what the Gospel *really* means for their life?

_____
_____
_____
_____
_____
_____
_____
_____
_____
_____
_____
_____
_____
_____
_____

CHAPTER 04
—

Abide or Depart

While the altar represents the moment of justification through Christ, it does not represent the life-long sanctification through relationship. In short, the altar is death, but it is also birth. It is the beginning of a relationship filled with commands, grace, conviction, mercy, and joy.

In the book of John, He tells those who already believed in Him, "…'If you abide in My word, you are My disciples indeed. And you shall know the truth, and the truth shall make you free.'" (John 8:31-32)

This statement sure seems deep. But in reality, Jesus is throwing us a softball. It's not very complex and there's not an attorney on the planet who would be confused about what Jesus is trying to say. If you do not abide in His Word, you are **not** His disciple. If you do not abide in His Word you will **not** know the truth (who is Jesus). If you do not abide in His Word you will **not** be set free. In simple terms, He's saying: abide or depart.

A passage this bold requires us to examine the definition of abiding. The Greek word is *meno*. It means to "continue in" or to "dwell in." It doesn't mean, "to choose to be present at one point in your life and then leave at another." It means to remain constantly, forever, until the day we go to be with the Lord.

What a request! What a contrast to how *we* have defined a disciple of Jesus. To put it briefly, the Western Church has not authenticated a Christian by their willingness to abide in God's Word, instead, they validate discipleship by how high you raise your hands during worship or how fervently you prayed in your small group or how often you serve in your church. Again, these common Christian expressions are not bad or sinful but they are different metrics of measurement than those of Jesus. Ultimately, the modern church sees genuine Christianity by spiritual activity instead of one's love for Christ shown through abiding in Him and His Word.

Now, as mentioned above spiritual activity is not wrong behavior. But spiritual activity without spiritual abiding is spiritual fraudulency. Jesus called these individuals hypocrites—which literally means *to act as if on stage*.

Our Lord is not looking for an act or self-righteous performance, He's looking for loyalty in relationship. In fact, throughout the gospels, Jesus says a resounding and repetitive statement: "If you love me, you will keep my commandments." In John chapter 14 alone, He says it four times (vs. 15, 21, 23, 24). Let me break His statement down to illustrate my point. Let's say that part one is "If you love me..." and part two is "... you will keep my commandments." This very statement demonstrates my argument beautifully—part one shows that relationship (love) must precede action (obedience). In other words, the greatest way to express your devotion to Him is not through spiritual activity. It's

"Jesus centralizes the path of showing Him our relational love by keeping His commandments."

#RealChristianity

Abide or Depart

not even through prayer, or preaching, or singing. Jesus centralizes the path of showing Him our relational love by **keeping His commandments.**

Now, Bible scholars will tell you that there are 1,050 commands in the New Testament for Christians to obey. Due to repetitions, you can distill them down to about 69 total commands. So, it begs the question, "In order to love Christ well, is He calling me to memorize these commands and obey them flawlessly?"

No. As the author of Hebrews reminds the early church of God's plan through the New Covenant, "This is the covenant that I will make with them after those days, says the Lord: I will put My laws into their hearts, and in their minds I will write them,'" (Hebrews 10:16).

God has given Christians like you and me, His Holy Spirit, the third Person of the Trinity, who prompts, convicts, and reminds us of these New Covenant commands. In truth, Jesus tells His disciples in John 14:26, "the Spirit will teach you all things, and bring to your remembrance all things that I said to you." Paul continues this theology in 1 Corinthians 2:12, "Now we have received, not the spirit of the world, but the Spirit who is from God, that we might know the things that have been freely given to us by God."

The Holy Spirit is our Helper to bring conviction and understanding of God and His ways. We need not worry about keeping a militant accuracy of the Old Testament Law or relying on our own strength to be righteous. Rather, we simply walk in the Spirit, work diligently to know God's Word, and remain faithful by abiding in our relationship with Christ. In doing these things, we will maintain our fellowship with the Spirit and in His grace, He will prompt us toward righteousness and conform us into the image of Jesus Christ.

Reflection Questions

How do you personally abide in Christ and His Word? List out a few examples from your own life below.

Do you centrally show your love for Christ by keeping His commandments, or have you adopted another spiritual means to express your core devotion to Him? Explain why you think Jesus has chosen keeping His commands as His preferred way to receive love from us.

_____
_____
_____
_____
_____
_____
_____
_____
_____
_____
_____
_____
_____
_____
_____
_____

CHAPTER 05

Do You Really Love Jesus?

I'd like to continue our discussion on love. Biblical love. In a culture and church who has handed over the work of defining ethics to our emotions, I believe it's essential to offer continued clarity on this fundamental virtue.

You can't love someone you don't know. Jesus understood this concept better than anyone else when he spoke what many Christians believe to be the most striking words in the New Testament:

> *"Not everyone who says to Me, 'Lord, Lord,' shall enter the kingdom of heaven, but he who does the will of My Father in heaven. Many will say to Me in*

> ***that day, 'Lord, Lord, have we not prophesied in Your name, cast out demons in Your name, and done many wonders in Your name?' And then I will declare to them, 'I never knew you; depart from Me, you who practice lawlessness!'*** —MATTHEW 7:21-32

For years, this passage frightened me. For some reason, Jesus denied these people's access into heaven. The people who were seemingly doing all the right spiritual things. The people who were prophesying for goodness sakes! They were casting out demons and doing many wonders in Jesus' name! But Jesus' response wasn't "Well-done, good and faithful servant." It was the exact opposite.

Jesus said to them, "I never knew you; depart from me you who practice lawlessness." What!? Lawlessness? At first glance, it doesn't appear that these Christians were practicing lawlessness. In fact, it looks like they're doing God's work!

Like me, you may find this passage concerning. If great works like prophesying, casting out demons, and doing

---

"Spiritual activity doesn't create spiritual security."

#RealChristianity

many wonders in Jesus' name ends with Him saying, "I never knew you..." then, what does it take to assure that Jesus does know us?

In his first epistle, the Apostle John gives us the direct answer—an answer that will further solidify the theme of the previous chapter and support the doctrine of this chapter.

> *"Now by this we know that we know Him, if we keep His commandments."* –1 JOHN 2:3

Pretty clear, right? But that's only half the story. Much like Jesus does, John issues a warning in the verses that follow:

> *"He who says, 'I know Him,' and does not keep His commandments, is a liar, and the truth is not in him. But whoever keeps His word, truly the love of God is perfected in him. By this we know that we are in Him."* –1 JOHN 2:4-5

I think the underlying lesson of this passage is this:

spiritual *activity* doesn't create spiritual *security*. It's not about how much worship music you sing. It's not about how powerful you can preach. It's not about how passionate you can pray. It's about building a real relationship with your Lord that is so overflowing with love that you order your life to prioritize His decrees. It's not about earning your salvation through works, it's about showing the evidence of your salvation through obedience. Ultimately, it's not about what you do. It's about your abundant love for Jesus because of what He's already done.

I believe Charles Spurgeon said it nicely, "Good works are not the root of faith, but they are its fruit."[4]

And this is where that group of spiritual people referenced in Matthew 7:21-32 made an eternal mistake. Instead of working from their salvation, they were working for it. Instead of showing the proof of their faith through good works, they hoped their good works were worthy of a saving hope in Christ.

As Christians, we must know deep in our bones that

we're not saved by our spiritual *activity*. We are saved because of our spiritual *standing*. You see, outside of Christ, we all practice lawlessness. Ephesians 2:1 tells us that outside of Christ we are, "dead in our trespasses and sins." The imagery here is of someone lying dead in a puddle of their own vomit and feces.

The prophet Isaiah reinforces this sureness of our depravity when he wrote, "But we are all like an unclean thing, and all our righteousnesses are like filthy rags." Paul, in his letter to the Romans, also chimes in on this reality when he references the words of King David in Romans 3:10, "There is none righteous, no, not one."

So how can you please God? If we're not righteous and even our "good" works aren't good to God, how does one seek the approval of their heavenly Father? How can we delight our Creator?

In Christ alone.

The truth is, outside of Christ, we are all guilty. Outside of Christ, we all deserve eternal separation from God.

"It's not about earning your salvation through works, it's about showing the evidence of your salvation through obedience."

#RealChristianity

Outside of Christ, we all have no hope. This is why the Gospel is so utterly beautiful. It's Good News because there is bad news. We are alive because we were dead. We are healed because we were sick. Not by our own works, but through our relationship with a worthy Christ—a gift of God (Ephesians 2:8-9).

This is grace, this is the source of our abundant joy, this is why we keep His commandments, this is why we're obedient and holy and humble, this is why we suffer for His name's sake.

So Christian, does He know you? Are you a sheep who hears His voice? Does His Spirit discipline you in error, quicken you to His will, comfort you through trial, and strengthen you in temptation? Are you standing on your own works? Or are your works evidence of you standing on His work?

We have a God who wants a relationship. We have a God who wants to dwell with us and in us. We have a God who wants more than activity, and information, and talent. He wants our hearts to bow to His Son. He wants a yielded, transformed, and regenerated child who seeks Him, listens to Him, and loves Him.

REFLECTION QUESTIONS

How do you know that you personally know Him?
How do you know that you love Him? Explain below.

Do you perform for God? Do you believe that something other than Christ alone makes God more happy with you? Are you working for God's approval in your own strength? If so, explain why?

CHAPTER 06

Costless Christianity

Boldness implies risk—a willingness to put something at stake. To be bold for Christ has historically cost much for many. In fact, the darker the culture, the higher the risk. The more hostile the environment, the more hazardous the witness.

For a variety of reasons, the church in the West has developed the idea that Christianity comes without a cost. In fact, many denominations have spun the Gospel into a relationship that comes only with material gain—from prosperity and healing to job promotions and success. They preach, "Follow Jesus and you'll live the abundant life you've always wanted!"

However, this theology isn't congruent with the Bible or church history. In the words of John Piper, "If God's love for His children is to be measured by our health, wealth, and comfort in this life, then God must have absolutely hated the Apostle Paul."[5]

Let's examine this further by looking at the life of the man God chose to reveal His Gospel to ends of the earth. In 2nd Corinthians 6:3-10 Paul describes his ministry in the following words (I've underlined for emphasis):

> *"We give no offense in anything, that our ministry may not be blamed. But in all things we commend ourselves as ministers of God: in much patience, in <u>tribulations, in needs, in distresses, in stripes, in imprisonments, in tumults, in labors, in sleeplessness, in fastings</u>; by purity, by knowledge, by longsuffering, by kindness, by the Holy Spirit, by sincere love, by the word of truth, by the power of God, by the armor of righteousness on the right hand and on the left, by honor and dishonor, by <u>evil report</u> and good report; <u>as deceivers</u>, and yet true; <u>as unknown</u>, and yet well known; <u>as dying</u>, and behold*

we live; <u>as chastened</u>, and yet not killed; <u>as sorrowful</u>, yet always rejoicing; <u>as poor</u>, yet making many rich; <u>as having nothing</u>, and yet possessing all things."

The truth is, following Christ does come at a cost. If it's not costing you, you would be wise to determine why. Now, hear me when I say this, I am not instructing you to go out and look for an expense to be paid. The Scriptures actually teach otherwise; we are to seek peace (Romans 12:8). But again, if your Christian life has created a pattern and history in which you have not encountered resistance, it may be worth introspection. After all, we are working against demonic powers and a defiant culture (Ephesians 6:12). Our message, The Gospel, is not solely one of good news, but also of grave news. I've offered a brief exposition of this message below:

> "YOU ARE A SINNER ENSLAVED TO YOUR SIN. AS A RESULT, YOU ARE SEPARATED FROM THE HOLY GOD WHO MADE YOU. HOWEVER, HE LOVES YOU AND WHILE YOU ARE CURRENTLY UNDER HIS WRATH, HE HAS PROVIDED A WAY TO ESCAPE HIS

"If God's love for His children is to be measured by our health, wealth, and comfort in this life then God absolutely hated the Apostle Paul."

#RealChristianity

ETERNAL CONSEQUENCES FOR YOUR REBELLION AGAINST HIM. YOU CAN BE REUNITED WITH YOUR GOD THROUGH REPENTANCE OF YOUR SIN, BELIEVING IN HIS SON JESUS CHRIST, MAKING HIM LORD, ACKNOWLEDGING HIS RESURRECTION, DYING TO YOUR OWN DESIRES, AND BEING BORN AGAIN OF THE SPIRIT OF GOD."

This is our anthem. This is the Gospel. In 1st Corinthians 1:18 Paul tells us how the world sees this Gospel.

> *"For the message of the cross is foolishness to those who are perishing, but to us who are being saved it is the power of God."*

Nevertheless, this is our commission (Matthew 28:16-20). This is our ministry—to bring the news of possible reconciliation to a rebellious people in hopes of facilitating peace between them and God through Christ (2nd Corinthians 5:18-19).

However, instead of embracing this ministry, many

churches and pastors have become expert dealers of a diluted Christianity. A Christ without a cross, forgiveness without repentance, heaven without hell, success without suffering, and health without illness.

In many ways, by withholding the full Gospel, we have vandalized and distorted the expectations of what it truly means to follow Jesus.

Jesus did not do this to His followers. In Matthew 10:16-22, we see Him doing the opposite. He actually cautions and prepares His disciples before sending them out into ministry with a sobering set of expectations.

> *"Behold, I send you out as sheep in the midst of wolves. Therefore be wise as serpents and harmless as doves. But beware of men, for they will deliver you up to councils and scourge you in their synagogues. You will be brought before governors and kings for My sake, as a testimony to them and to the Gentiles. But when they deliver you up, do not worry about how or what you should speak. For it will be given to you in that hour what you should speak; for it is not you who speak,*

but the Spirit of your Father who speaks in you. 'Now brother will deliver up brother to death, and a father his child; and children will rise up against parents and cause them to be put to death. And you will be hated by all for My name's sake. But he who endures to the end will be saved.'"

The Gospel is offensive not because it's insulting. It's offensive because it's condemning of those who choose not to believe that Jesus is the Christ (John 3:18). The message that *real* Christians are called to carry turns men into wolves because of the doom that is indicated by its denial.

As a matter of fact, this passage tells us that the opposition that Christians are to expect in their ministry is to be so fierce that for some it will break the barriers of familial love. While many may not believe that the affection of those relations found within the family could be severed to such an extent, history sadly reminds us that this vicious reality is possible. What evidence of man's need for Christ!

The Gospel is offensive not because it's insulting. It's offensive because it's condemning of those who choose not to believe that Jesus is the Christ.

#RealChristianity

Albert Barnes, an American theologian of the 1800's penned a dreadfully graphic commentary on this passage. The rawness of its contents compelled me to pray if it should be included in this manuscript. To that end, I have determined that it is edifying for our present discussion:

> *"Nothing else but this dreadful opposition to God and His gospel ever has induced or ever can induce people to violate the most tender relations, and consign the best of friends to torture, racks, and flames. History adds to the horrors of this, that those who were put to death in persecution were tormented in the most awful modes that human ingenuity could devise. They were crucified; were thrown into boiling oil; were burned at the stake; were roasted slowly over coals; were compelled to drink melted lead; were torn in pieces by beasts of prey; were covered with pitch and set on fire. Yet, dreadful as this prediction was, it was fulfilled; and, incredible as it seems, parents and children, husbands and wives, were found wicked enough to deliver up each other to these cruel modes of death on account of attachment to the gospel."* [6]

What a foreign experience to the church in the West which seemingly lives under the unsaid philosophy of "If we just present Jesus correctly, everyone will realize how much He loves them and they will finally love Him back."

It's as if we believe that having the right graphic design, the most emotional worship songs, and the best quotable sermon series will finally convince the onlooking public that Jesus is not offensive to the desires of mankind.

Somehow, we forget that Jesus represented Jesus better than anyone could represent Jesus and even He got Himself killed for it. Somehow, we forget that the Bible even testifies that Jesus is, "A stone of stumbling; And a rock of offense." (1st Peter 2:8).

Now, my goal is not to paint a commitment to Christ as a heavy and burdensome relationship. No. My mission is to illuminate the biblical results of those who represent the *real* Christ and to allow us each to examine if there are any gaps between the results of *our* lives and the Bible's assured claims for those who bear the true Gospel.

For example, in Paul's second letter to Timothy, we see yet again this confirmation of opposition so absent in the Western Church.

> ***"Yes, and all who desire to live godly in Christ Jesus will suffer persecution."*** –2 TIMOTHY 3:12

Now, it's easy to believe that the reason Western Christians may not be experiencing these resistant outcomes in their ministries is due to the blessings of religious freedom granted through governance, or because of the civility of a modern culture. However, I don't believe this is a reliable hypothesis. While the United States has surely shielded the opportunities of mass scale persecution with its current Constitution, I believe the majority of the persecution warned of in the Scriptures is regarding the interpersonal relationships of small communities, not the rare, wide-spread genocidal form we see scattered throughout history.

In other words, the form of persecution common to all Christians in all times typically derives from a brother or sister who is willing to lovingly and gently speak the Truth of God into a circumstance or relationship. That is, when a Christian refuses to compromise God's Word for the comfort of those who may be listening. In addition, we also see persecution around politically charged issues from abortion and sexuality, to gender and parental rights. Any territory in which God's ways come in conflict with the culture, the Christian who is willing to speak is liable to experience the persecutory promises of Scripture.

Sadly, many Christians, however, are found sitting where God calls them to stand. They are found silent when God called for a speaker.

Edmund Burke's words from the eighteenth century are a timely rebuke for many of today's passive Christians,

> *"The only thing necessary for the triumph of evil is for good men to do nothing."* [7]

We are not lacking persecution in the West because persecution doesn't exist, we're lacking persecution because we're not standing for truth worthy of persecution.

#RealChristianity

Ultimately, what you remain silent about, you permit. We, as Christians, must be careful that the fear of man isn't forcing us to cower on matters where God calls for courage.

Bottom line, we are not lacking persecution in the West because persecution doesn't exist, we're lacking persecution because we're not standing for truth worthy of persecution.

I'll close with the words of our Lord on this matter as I believe it will bring clarity on how Jesus instructs us to view these afflictions. Let it be a hymn to your heart, a fortitude in your fear, and a battle cry in your pursuit of peace and love.

> *"Blessed are those who are persecuted for righteousness' sake, For theirs is the kingdom of heaven. Blessed are you when they revile and persecute you, and say all kinds of evil against you falsely for My sake. Rejoice and be exceedingly glad, for great is your reward in heaven, for so they persecuted the prophets who were before you."* —MATTHEW 5:10-12

Are you willing to be blessed in this matter? Can you rejoice in the midst of such opposition? Boldness comes with a cost. Christ comes with a cost. But great is your reward in heaven.

Reflection Questions

Are you bold enough to be a threat to the enemy? Have you experienced persecution or been forced to pay a price (relationally, financially, bodily) for following Christ? Please explain below.

Have you experienced affliction as a result of your willingness to stand for truth in a culture of lies or do you typically stay silent on difficult and costly topics? Explain below.

CHAPTER 07

Eternally Secure or Relationally Contingent?

It's dangerous to be bold in your witness without being accurate in your theology. Many workers are currently in the field sowing unhealthy seeds with disfigured doctrine and wondering why their fruit is bitter. We must remember that there is only one Gospel. Therefore, it's critical that we each understand the mechanics of this Gospel that we might live it faithfully, defend it intellectually, and present it accurately.

Now, like many components of the Gospel, there is tension and debate within the church. There are passages which have caused sectarianism, denominations, and even cold-hearted divisions.

That said, I want to look at one debate in particular which, I believe sets the heart and rhythm for how a believer walks out their daily relationship with Christ.

It's one of the loudest and most consuming of debates in the church today. Can you walk away from your faith or not? You may have heard it as the "once saved, always saved" theology—a philosophy made popular through John Calvin's theory of the "Preservation of the Saints." It's the classic discussion between predestination and free will.

As I already mentioned, it's utterly critical that we understand the Bible's multi-dimensional position on this matter as it will affect how you view your relationship with Christ, the security of your salvation, and your understanding of the Gospel.

Now, we can spend chapters upon chapters on this issue alone, but I have chosen to simplify my personal position for the sake of your sanity.

I think Chad Bird outlines this theology succinctly. He

writes, "In the Bible, I see two true doctrines:

1. **ONCE YOU ARE A BELIEVER IN CHRIST, YOUR SALVATION IS FOREVER SECURE IN HIM.**

2. **ONCE YOU ARE A BELIEVER IN CHRIST, YOU CAN LATER REJECT HIS SALVATION THROUGH REBELLION.**

To us, these may appear to be mutually exclusive. Either number one is true or number two is true, but they can't both be true."[8]

However, the Scriptures cite both (hence the great debate).

The sensed tension between them is man's intellectual struggle between God's two words to us: the word of promise and the word of warning. In other words, we are eternally secure if we are relationally engaged.

While a Calvinist will disagree with me on this point, allow me to further solidify my position. If God is love (1 John 4:8) then love must offer the choice to disbelieve. If we cannot walk away from our faith, then we aren't in a loving relationship—we are in a compliant relationship. The truth is, just like you and I can choose to walk away from our marriage, or our children, or our career, we can choose to walk away from Christ.

But I can hear it now, "Doesn't the Bible say that nothing can snatch us out of His hand? Doesn't it also say that nothing can separate us from the love of Christ?" It does. And I agree with these passages. But together, let's examine what they are actually saying.

> *"My sheep hear My voice, and I know them, and they follow Me. And I give them eternal life, and they shall never perish; neither shall anyone snatch them out of My hand. My Father, who has given them to Me, is greater than all; and no one is able to snatch them out of My Father's hand."* –JOHN 10:27-29

Now let's look at Romans 8:35-39

> *"Who shall separate us from the love of Christ? Shall tribulation, or distress, or persecution, or famine, or*

nakedness, or peril, or sword? ...Yet in all these things we are more than conquerors through Him who loved us. For I am persuaded that neither death nor life, nor angels nor principalities nor powers, nor things present nor things to come, nor height nor depth, nor any other created thing, shall be able to separate us from the love of God which is in Christ Jesus our Lord."

I want to draw your attention to what many Christians miss in these passages. First, notice in the passage seen in the book of John that the sheep hear, they are known, and they follow. A follower is never forced to follow or to continue following. If they were, then they would not be followers but slaves. Secondly, both Christ and Paul are making a case that no *external* thing can steal you away from Christ's salvation and love. However, these passages do not support the idea that no *internal* thing can take you away from your relationship and salvation in Christ.

The point I'm making is this: We have free will. We can, out of His love for us, leave. Now, is God sovereign? Absolutely. Any Christian who denies the sovereignty

---

Because God loves us, He will never force us to stay in a relationship with Him. It is something that we must continue to choose.

#RealChristianity

of God cannot be in agreement with Scripture. That said, any Christian who rejects personal responsibility is also in conflict with Scripture. The narrative of the Bible holds both of these truths in balance. A common example is seen when Paul tells the Philippians 2:12 to, "Work out your own salvation with fear and trembling" which highlights *our* responsibility. In the very next verse, it says, "for it is God who works in you both to will and to do for His good pleasure" which highlights the sovereignty of God. This bilateral relationship between God's sovereignty and man's free will is painted across the Scriptures.

Now to close my previous point, for those in Christ, our salvation cannot be altered by any other person or outside thing—no exterior entity or power can steal us from His hand. But because God loves us, He will never force us to stay in a relationship with Him. It is something that we must continue to choose.

I think Jesus makes this concept of relational choice abundantly clear throughout the Gospels. Let's briefly look at His words found in John 15:5-8 (I've underlined for emphasis).

> *"I am the vine, you are the branches. <u>He who</u> abides in Me, and I in him, bears much fruit; for without Me you can do nothing. <u>If</u> anyone <u>does not</u> abide in Me, he is cast out as a branch and is withered; and they gather them and throw them into the fire, and they are burned. <u>If</u> you abide in Me, and My words abide in you, you will ask what you desire, and it shall be done for you. By this My Father is glorified, that you bear much fruit; so you will be My disciples."*

First, the underlined phrases assert the idea that there is a possibility of not choosing to abide in Him. Specifically, the word "if" implies a contingency clause. It suggests that there is an option for us to participate, or not.

Secondly, the text calls those who are cast out "branches" and that they "wither." This could imply that these individuals at one point were connected to the vine. But now, in their choice to not abide have been cast out and their life is now dried up (see Matthew 13:18-23). Ultimately, this indicates that our relationship with Christ isn't robotic or forced, it is organic and voluntary.

Ravi Zacharias, in an article he wrote in the 1980s, offered a beautiful example that may help us to understand and embrace the tension between God's sovereignty and man's free will. He writes:

> *"The sovereignty and responsibility issue should really be seen as two opposite poles of the same position. Light, for example, is viewed from some vantage points as particles. From other vantage points, it is viewed as waves. Scientists are aware that light could not be both particles and waves, so they have coined a term for it, a kind of a construct, and they call it a "photon." All they have done is create a word and a category that accommodates both perspectives which are real. I think you should view the sovereignty of God and the responsibility of man as a kind of a precious stone with two facets to it. When it catches the light from one direction, you see one color; when it catches the light from the other direction you see the other color."[9]*

Humans love to systematize the Bible in an attempt to eliminate ambiguity and mystery. More than that, we like to define these systems by giving them names; and anyone who does not align and adopt those names, are wrong. In some way, those who embrace a fixed, systematic theology are stating that they, as finite beings, have fully understood an infinite God. In my opinion, it is rooted in pride and lacking a sincere desire to embrace the profound complexities of our Creator.

Now, please do not equate my thesis for *choosing* relationship as an argument for works-based salvation. I am not saying that we must continue to perform or that we are redeemed through our own efforts. I'm saying if we want a saving relationship with Christ we must continue to choose to pursue a faith-centered relationship with Christ.

There is not a relationship in existence in which withdrawing or stagnancy does not seriously damage the bond of the two parties. A relationship requires consistent strengthening of its linkage, or it withers to the point of dissolution.

Here's why this matters, people who have walked with the Lord for many years, who have served in missions, who have led worship at church, who have preached from the pulpit, and who have prayed fervently have *chosen* to stop pursuing Christ and as a result has allowed their faith to die altogether. Now, you might respond with the all too anticipated, "Well then they weren't actually saved in the first place" argumentation. And that's fair. After all, 1st John 2:19 seems to validate that logic quite nicely.

> *"They went out from us, but they were not of us; for if they had been of us, they would have continued with us; but they went out that they might be made manifest, that none of them were of us."*

And there's the loop that creates the debate on two sides of that stone. The friction found between many of the greatest theologians of all time—were they saved and walked away or never saved in the first place? For many years, this debate caused me much spiritual frustration.

But today, I no longer care about the debate and neither should you. Here's why...

This entire theological battlefield is not useful for the vast majority of Christians. Why? Because God isn't interested in us seeking to know how far we can stray without losing our salvation. He's not even interested in how secure we can become through Bible information. What God is interested in is a vibrant relationship where we abide in Him, seek His Kingdom, pick up our cross daily, love one another, walk in the Spirit, and make Him Lord.

Ultimately, the debate doesn't help *you* evaluate *your* personal standing with God.

But there is something we can learn from it. We must remember that those followers of Christ throughout history, who have left the faith, whether by backsliding, or by choice, or by doubt or by sin, all believed they were saved at one point.

Many had read books like this one. Some had graduated

from seminary. Droves went to church regularly. In other words, every person who left Christ was at one point much like you and me. Just like nobody plans for divorce on their wedding day, no follower of Christ plans for their departure during their reception of the Gospel.

So the value of this entire debate is not found within the camps of theology that determine who is saved or not saved. The value in this debate is in knowing what the Bible says about those who *are* saved.

To this understanding, we can examine ourselves. To this understanding, we can determine if we are in a faithful relationship with Christ. To this understanding, we can conclude if we're in His will. To this understanding, we can confirm if we're *really* Christian.

This is helpful. This takes our eyes off the argument and puts them back on us. This takes our focus off knowing where the line is or isn't and puts it back on Christ.

Do not worry about your salvation. Seek Christ. Do not

be careless in your relationship with God. Seek Christ. Do not rest in Calvinism or Arminianism or any other systematic theology, rest in Christ.

Debates are a part of the Christian life, but no debate will ever offer more security than simply pursuing a deep, committed, reciprocal relationship with Christ.

Reflection Questions

How do you view your salvation? Do you believe that you are saved and can never not be saved no matter what you do? Or do you believe you are saved because you are in a Gospel relationship with Christ?

_____

_____

_____

_____

_____

_____

_____

_____

_____

_____

_____

_____

_____

_____

_____

_____

If you treated your spouse, or child, or parents the way you treat your relationship with Christ would they say you're in a deep and loving relationship or a stagnant and diminishing relationship? Explain below.

CHAPTER 08

Hate the Captor, Not the Captive

The gap between morality and immorality is quickly gaining distance in our world. By even mentioning the idea of an unchanging moral code it makes society cringe. And that's exactly why there's so much conflict between culture and Christ.

As a Christian, you're entering a battlefield where God and the world are at war. You may not have asked to be included in the crossfire, but by simply aligning yourself with His Word and following His commandments, you're inviting flaming arrows from the enemy into your life.

Paul, in his letter to the Ephesians brings clarity to the type of conflict Christians are to expect: "For we do not wrestle against flesh and blood, but against principalities, against powers, against the rulers of the darkness of this age, against spiritual hosts of wickedness in the heavenly places" (Ephesians 6:12). You see, we're not fighting the captive. We're fighting the captor—the enemy, the demonic realm—and it's a tough fight.

In their boldness, many Christians have become targets—wounded, weakened, and scarred. To this, I must remind us all of Paul's words to the risk-taking, persecuted church in Rome. He says, "Let love be without hypocrisy. Abhor what is evil. Cling to what is good" (Romans 10:9).

Put in context, the culture's hostile conditions don't excuse Christians from the responsibility to love their neighbor and cling to what is good. In the Gospel of Matthew, Jesus even goes as far as to say, "You have heard that it was said, 'You shall love your neighbor and hate your enemy.' But I say to you, love your enemies,

———————

The culture's hostile conditions don't excuse Christians from the responsibility to love their neighbor and cling to what is good.

#RealChristianity

bless those who curse you, do good to those who hate you, and pray for those who spitefully use you and persecute you."

Ultimately, Jesus is establishing the age-old idea, "Hate the sin but love the sinner." As trite as that might sound to a Christian who has heard it a thousand times—the church might need to hear it a thousand more.

I don't want to mislead you in all this. Satan is diligent at increasing confusion, fruitlessness, and distance. He's seared the hearts and consciences of many in the church. And while the culture will attack you for following Christ, I want you to see where these arrows are flying from and help you to avoid getting hit.

There are over 100 scriptures in the New Testament alone that speak to this topic (many were discussed in chapter six). Jesus in the book of John says, "Remember the word that I said to you, 'A servant is not greater than his master.' If they persecuted Me, they will also persecute you."

It should be no shock that the closer you get to Christ the more the culture will hate you. And this means that being bold for Christ in an anti-Christian world will require you to constantly walk in the Spirit. It will require you to be holy as He is holy. And it will require you to do everything we've already learned in this book.

When you do these things, you will be able to deflect many of these flaming arrows. You will be able to endure your time in this war. However, it does not mean that we accept evil or become numb to its results. In fact, Proverbs 8:13 says, "The fear of the Lord is to hate evil."

So, how are we supposed to deal with evil? More than that, how do we deal with people who are evil and walk in wickedness and opposition to the Lord? In other words, how do we fight in the battle between culture and Christ?

I'll begin with what Paul instructs in the book of Romans.

> ***Repay no one evil for evil. Have regard for good things in the sight of all men. If it is possible, as much as depends on you, live peaceably with all men. Beloved, do not avenge yourselves, but rather give place to wrath; for it is written, "Vengeance is Mine, I will repay," says the Lord. Therefore "If your enemy is hungry, feed him; If he is thirsty, give him a drink; For in so doing you will heap coals of fire on his head." Do not be overcome by evil, but overcome evil with good.'* —ROMANS 12:17-21**

Returning hate to hateful people is not God's solution. It's love. It's goodness and righteousness and kindness. Jesus calls us to a counterintuitive relationship with an adverse world. A journey where up is down, last is first, and weak is strong. A journey where we bless those who curse us and pray for those who hurt us. A journey where, at our own martyrdom, we are to plead with Christ for the forgiveness of our killers.

What I want you to see here is that *real* Christianity is about indescribable and unfathomable love. We see this in Stephen at the time of his death (Acts 7:60).

We see it in quantity in the Hall of Faith (Hebrews 11) where God's people show love in the midst of fatal persecution. But most of all, we see it in Christ on the cross when He prays the words for his captors, "Father, forgive them, for they do not know what they do" (Luke 23:34).

Now, statistically, most of us will not experience martyrdom. Be we will all experience mistreatment. As a Christian, you're not walking into a safe house. You're walking into war. You're a soldier who God is going to use in the fight against Satan and the restoration of humanity. It's going to be difficult. It's going to be hard.

We know this because as Paul writes to Timothy he says, "You therefore must endure hardship as a good soldier of Jesus Christ" (1 Timothy 2:3). But as I mentioned in chapter six, there's no such thing as costless Christianity. Jesus isn't interested in Christians who aren't willing to forsake everything to follow Him (Luke 14:33). He's not interested in sign-me-up Christians who aren't prepared to make the beautiful, yet difficult sacrifices down the road. He's interested in

---

As a Christian, you're not walking into a safe house. You're walking into war.

#RealChristianity

faithful travelers, the feet of those who carry Gospel, and men and women with the spiritual heart of a Lion.

THE BEAUTIFUL, DIFFICULT, UPHILL ROAD

In my experience, Christians who are puzzled by the world around them simply haven't taken the time to read, study, and know God and His word. As you begin to understand the grand narrative of the Bible all the brokenness in our culture becomes quite clear.

That said, in these last days, it has become more complex to navigate. Fuzziness is being added atop of fogginess and we are beginning to see the emerging apostate church. The captor is aware of God's timeline and he's advancing his tactics. A.W. Tozer once said, "The devil is a better theologian than any of us."[10] His desperation is revealing itself in the state of the Western Church—from the far-reaching prosperity gospel and the sexual sin-accepting progressive church to the cults of Mormonism and the Jehovah's Witnesses, heresy is all around us.

The book of Revelation calls this emerging "church" "the

harlot" or "the scarlet." These are just poetic names for the cheating bride of Christ. They're not real Christians. They're deceived believers of a false gospel—a form of godliness without the power (2 Timothy 3:5). You may have already noticed the Christ-less doctrines of this harlot church manifesting in some churches in your own city. You may have even noticed it in your own church. However, it's something we are not to be surprised by. For Scripture tells us these days are coming:

> *"For the time will come when they will not endure sound doctrine, but according to their own desires, because they have itching ears, they will heap up for themselves teachers; and they will turn their ears away from the truth, and be turned aside to fables."*
> −2 TIMOTHY 4:3-4

Unfortunately, the captor's work is not something bound to the outer places. His work can and has seeped into the walls of the church—distorting God's Truth and leading many astray. The lesson is this: distinguishing between the culture and the church has been an easier task for much of recent history. Today, those groups have become more challenging to properly discern. However, that passage in 2nd Timothy teaches us that those who are not God's people will always reveal themselves by not embracing God's Word. On the contrary, the embracing of God's Word will always be the evidence of God's people.

Years ago, I was driving my daughter up a 7,200-foot mountain to our cabin in Lake Arrowhead, California. I remember her asking, in a seemingly frustrated tone, if the road was going to be uphill and winding the entire way. I responded with, "Yes, Aria. Yes, it is. But let's focus on how beautiful it is instead."

I think Christianity is similar. This side of heaven, it's uphill and winding. It seems like it's never getting easier and the journey just keeps climbing. There are turns and cliffs all around us and the higher you get the harder you fall.

Even still, it's marvelous. An enchanting adventure—a plot filled with a King to serve, an enemy to overcome, and a people to love. It's strenuous and weighty but there's no better road out there.

REFLECTION QUESTIONS

We often blame God for the evil in the world, and we often blame the captive for the works of the captor. Are you properly placing your grievances to the one who is the author of evil, or have you become bitter with God or the people who have hurt you?

It's critical that we don't over-spiritualize or under-spiritualize the problems and blessings in our lives. The Scriptures teach us to be sober minded in all things. That said, how do you see spiritual warfare played out in your life? Explain below.

CONCLUSION
—

Real Christianity

After reading a book like this, it's easy to believe that following Christ is more difficult than enjoyable. To pay a price for our beliefs, to abide in His Word, to maintain a faith-based relationship, to take The Scriptures as truth, to keep His commandments, to endure persecution, and to return good for evil. At first glance, this seems like a life of overwhelming discipline and diligence. But let's look at this idea for a moment.

What's more difficult? Following God's ways or embracing our own? What's more dangerous? Walking in His precepts or indulging in the culture's? You see, every time we think that life will be better by breaking

We must realize that it is not God who reaps the reward of obedience to His ways, it's us. We are the beneficiaries of obedience to God, not Him!

#RealChristianity

God's laws, we must remember that we don't just break God's laws—we also break ourselves. We must realize that it is not God who reaps the reward of obedience to His ways, it's us. We are the beneficiaries of obedience to God, not Him!

In a very practical way, God's laws exist to protect us against sin and brokenness. If you think walking in the Spirit is difficult, if you think walking in purity is difficult, if you think that being sober is difficult, if you think being mature is difficult, if you think that studying the Bible is difficult, I promise you that the alternatives lead you to a life that is **far more** difficult.

I think of the story found toward the end of John chapter six. Jesus just finished preaching on a difficult topic. A topic that was so difficult that many of His disciples decide to leave.

> *"From that time many of His disciples went back and walked with Him no more. Then Jesus said to the twelve, 'Do you also want to go away?' But Simon Peter answered Him, 'Lord, to whom shall we go? You*

> *have the words of eternal life. Also we have come to believe and know that You are the Christ, the Son of the living God.'" —JOHN 6:66-69*

I love Peter's response. He realized that regardless of how tough it might seem to follow Jesus, if he abandoned Him, he would be in an even tougher position. He says, "To whom shall we go?" You see, Peter knew the truth that was written in Acts 4:11–12, "This is the stone which was rejected by you builders, which has become the chief cornerstone. Nor is there salvation in any other, for there is no other name under heaven given among men by which we must be saved."

As Christians, we must believe that the safest and most joyful place we will ever be is under the instruction of Jesus Christ and His Word. Every time we move out from under His will and His ways, life will get harder, more confusing, and painful.

Ultimately, in classic counterintuitive fashion, God makes it clear that *real* Christianity, while it is not the path most traveled, it is certainly the path of least

---

Real Christianity, while it is not the path most traveled, it is certainly the path of least resistance.

#RealChristianity

resistance. It is a path of purpose and love and security and power and rest.

I will close with the words of our Lord in Matthew 11:28–30, "Come to Me, all you who labor and are heavy laden, and I will give you rest. Take My yoke upon you and learn from Me, for I am gentle and lowly in heart, and you will find rest for your souls. For My yoke is easy and My burden is light."

Let us come to our Lord in confidence. Let us believe that His ways will give us the most peace, the most rest, the most security, the most joy, and the most fruitful life available this side of heaven.

An Important Note
for the Church

RELEARN CHURCH
—

Bringing the Church Back to the Bible

I believe much of the doctrinal naivety and biblical illiteracy among Christians in the West is merely a result of how we have chosen to do church.

Because we have converted the meeting of the saints almost solely into the outward work of evangelism, we have largely limited the more advanced and mature doctrines of Scripture from the pulpit.

In fact, in our efforts to meet the needs of the lost through evangelism, we have actually failed to meet the needs of the saved through doctrine. As a result, we have a thin church, starving on meager rations of truth. Ultimately, the Western Church is spiritually immature because we have made our time together on Sunday centrally about the visitors and, in doing so, have neglected the spiritual growth of the committed.

But there's so much more.

Millions of Christians are leaving the institutional church on a search for Jesus. They are Gospel believing nomads homesick for deep and committed missional community. They are longing to be discipled and spiritually parented by mature men and women of the cross. They are craving the unabridged and rich truths of the Bible. But most of all, they want their church experience to match up with the explosive, vibrant, and powerful Christian account they see in the New Testament.

To this need, Veronica and I have been called. Called to bring the church back to the Bible. Called to restore the Scripture's original design for the church meeting. Called to teach Christians how to establish fruitful, thriving, Spirit-filled, Gospel-centered communities.

To this, we labor. From books like the one you're reading to podcasts, articles, and online curriculum, it's our mission to help thousands of Christians unlearn much of what they've experienced and relearn church according to the Bible.

If you're interested in learning more about our ministry, planting a biblical church, or supporting our efforts financially, you can do so at RelearnChurch.org.

Back to the Bible,

Dale Partridge, President
RelearnChurch.org

ENDNOTES

1 "Washer, Paul." Audio Format. Made available by Sermon Audio: www.sermonaudio.com/sermon/831101319581.

2 "Youssef, Michael." *The Hidden Enemy*. 2018. Published by Tyndale House Publishers, Inc., Carol Stream, IL.

3 "A Quote by Booker T. Washington." Goodreads, Goodreads, www.goodreads.com/quotes/9580325-a-lie-doesn-t-become-truth-wrong-doesn-t-become-right-and.

4 "Spurgeon, Charles." *The Complete Works of C. H. Spurgeon*, Volume 48: Sermons 2760 to 2811.

5 "John Piper Quote." AZ Quotes, www.azquotes.com/quote/1318240.

6 "Barnes, Albert." *Notes, Explanatory and Practical, on the Gospels:* Designed for ..., Volume 1. 1855 by Harper & Brothers Publishers.

7 "Edmund Burke Quotes." BrainyQuote, Brainy Quote, www.brainyquote.com/quotes/edmund_burke_377528.

8 "Bird, Chad." "Once Saved, Always Saved: True or Not?" 1517, 2017, 2017, www.1517.org/articles/once-saved-always-saved-true-or-not.

9 "Web Author." "Why Ravi Zacharias Rejects Calvinism." SOTERIOLOGY 101, 16 Feb. 2018, soteriology101.com/2017/06/16/why-ravi-zacharias-rejects-calvinism/.

10 "Tozer, A.W. Section: Devil." Who Said That?; More than 2,500 Usable Quotes and Illustrations, by George Sweeting, Word, 1995.

NOTES

Made in the USA
Middletown, DE
30 January 2020

83949215R00089